A Book of Personal Feelings
Through Poetry
by

Edith P. A. Follett

To my wonderful and extraordinary
husband

Randolph G. Follett

Whose inspiration and drive made

This book possible.

Index

Quotes: Unknown, Edgar Allen Poe, Frederick Douglass, Jim Rohn, Martin Luther,

Life

"You can close your eyes to things you don't want to see, but you can't close your heart to the things you don't want to feel."

- Unknown

He Sits and Stares

My father sits and stares
As we move to and fro on tip toe
He never lets us know what he's
    thinking
As he turns in his chair

As a statue in constant solitude he sits,
    he turns his head away
Portly and stern as a man made of clay
He sits stiff and tense all day

We sit and stare at him, prompting him
    to stir.
Now and then as he takes a breath, we
    watch him stiffen in his chair
As he declares, "So, this is how a
goldfish fairs".

Under The Banyan Tree

All day long I swing

Between the banyan trees

Catching the beams of light

Dancing on through the leaves

Swinging and flying up into the air

Getting my mom to push me

Higher and higher each time

I love to swing on my swing

Swinging as high as I can

Under the banyan tree

Grandma's Dilemma

What a noise there is today
Waking every day with noise
In my ears, all around up and down
Never ending, never stopping
Singing jumping shouting even
clucking

Then the quiet, oh the awful quiet
For a few hours of quiet
The quiet is deafening, what's wrong!
She's what's wrong, she's gone.

Waiting, waiting, waiting
Until two what shall I do?
Until I hear again that wonderful
   noise
HI, GRANMA!
Then it starts again
The noise, the noise, the noise.

The Balloons

Let go the string
Let them go
They will hover above
Until they are blown away
Let go the string

Way up in the sky they go
Blue, red, yellow and green
For all of us to see
Let go the string

Be brave let them go
You cannot hold on forever
They are blown to fly
High in the sky

Yes, she will cry
But she must understand
she was born to fly
Let go the string.

How Long Is Forever

How long is forever?
Do we really know?
As the time we are allotted
Should we want to know?

How long is forever?
Someone has to see
Do we set our sights on high or too
    low to know?

How long is forever?
Should we even ask?
What it's really all about
Or how much oats to sow?

How long is forever?
I don't really care
And even if I did
I don't like to share

The Birds

Seen from my window
Little birds flurrying by
With feathers gold and black
Fluttering through my mango tree

They twitter and flutter
Feeding on its fruit
Each limb holds goodness
Mangos sweet and juicy

They taste as they go
No intruders here will taste this trees
    sweet nectar
On pain of bitter beak

On this sunny day
They suddenly flew away
What could make them stay?
Not even the sweet nectar of my
mango tree

Insanity

"I became insane, with long
   intervals of horrible sanity".

Edgar Allan Poe

Put Away

I, will not be put away from your
    mind or sight

You're mine and mine alone, come to
    me now

Don't make me call again; you are so
    used to pain

Again I call, you hold me, at bay?

See my gentle hand; see my hand
    around your neck so tight

Come without a fight, I squeeze with
    all my might and stare without
    sight into the night

Let me go! Let me go! I will not be
    put away!

See, it was she; she would not come
    to me

The Hiding Place

In the cave of my mind
I could not find
A light to guide me home

Deep in my mind I sit cold and alone
In the center of my skull
Waiting for the light

I peep out once and a while
And withdraw further into my hiding
    place
Following the dark tunnels and twisted
    lanes

My hiding place gives me a place to go
    when things don't go my way
To hide and reappear when the light
    chooses

Where is the light, I thought I saw?
Blink again for me to see and follow
Or I will forever be here alone
In my hiding place.

The Fan

Every hour of every day, I think of
  you here
Every minute of every day, I need
  you with me
These feelings of mine go beyond all
  reason or rhyme
As I have never spoken to you of my
  reality

My whole being understands that this
  cannot be real
But I am still consumed with my
  need for you
I need to hear your voice, feel your
  soft embrace
I must taste the sweetness of your
  tender soft moist mouth.
Feel the warmth of your body lying
  close to mine

I long to feel the rhythmic heaving of
  our bodies in unison
My heart imagines your every touch
  and your every action

The Fan

Whilst we lie together alone,
    uninterrupted in each other's arms
I am crazed with these images of our
    unconsummated love

We make love in my mind's eye with
    every thrust
Hot, deep and hard as your back arches
    its commands
I cannot unwind my mind from your tall
    form
Nor tear my eyes away from your hard
    lean body

Smoldering blue eyes and the shy tilt of
    your head
Draw me closer to your every need or
    intended motion
Closer and with intent, I become your
    ultimate imaginary slave
Yearning for your touch, your smell, and
    every whimsical need

My mind is made up, I must fight this
    insanity

Why?

Why is my heart so angry and my
tears subdued?

Now that I'm without you

Tell me if this is my due?

Why do I not reveal myself to you?

Why do I not let you see me?

Why have I never opened my heart?

Why do my lips utter words of
harshness, suspicion and confusion

Why do I stare without seeing?

Why are my arms empty?

Why are they not around you?

Wake up I'm talking to you

By The Lake Of Time

By the lake of time I wonder
Searching for my reflection in the cool
    crystal waters
Dipping my toes here and there
Hoping to catch sight of my mortality
Unable to pinpoint the beginning or the
    end of my existence

Slipping and splashing trying to make
    some semblance of my life
I catch a glimpse of my reflection
Yet again, my task eludes me as it slips
    out of sight
A sliver of memory jumps out, and is
    placed in a pool beside me, the
    swirling stops

Bending, I peer into the time capsule
    that was once my life.
Swearing beneath my breath
As it disappears under the glistening
    green embankment
How could I have been so blind?
To believe I could hold on to that
    passage of time?

Struggle

"Without a struggle, there can be no progress".

Frederick Douglass

Can't Say Goodbye

I could never say goodbye to you again

Not even to ease the pain.

Beloved, see me again

As a vision in my brain

You make me insane

I could never say goodbye to you again

Sometimes

Sometimes when I'm alone I think of
all the things I've done
Sometimes alone in the dark I
consider all the things I should
have done
Things I regret, things I should forget
In order to forgive myself

Sometimes when I'm alone
My thoughts go back in time
And I debate on what I should have
done
Should I be so conscious of all these
things, I should forget?
What can I do to let go of these
feelings I regret?

Sometimes when I am alone in the
dark
I think of what I should have done
but didn't
Feelings of regret wash over me,
submerge me, holding me tightly
by my neck

She Stands

She stands erect, as the young do
Shoulders squared, arms stiff, fists
    clenched
Stoutly she battles all odds, from one
    day to the next

She navigates her way through the
    universe
Stepping aside when she can
Taking on all comers if she can't

Her eyes fastened on her prize
Her stance shifts to take on her next
    task.

Life! And all it has to offer,
Sprawls out before her, with roads
    that interlace
Prancing in and out of all boundaries
With changes and choices, only she
    can make
She steps in, out and up facing the
    world,
As she follows the life, she has
    chosen

Let Me Sleep

Oh leave me be
Let me sleep
My head is aching even as we speak

My toes tingle.
My breath is less than fresh
I can't even roll over onto my chest

My eyes won't open
As the eyelids are stuck quite shut
Leave me be
Let me sleep

My stomach now aches from a
    newfound hunger
Wait, I have to lie down to make a
    number?

Oh, here comes my coffee
No need for slumber
I'll drink it right here
Here under my covers

The Family Man

Work for my family
Work for bills
Never ending never stopping
The years go by
Without a thought

Money comes, money goes
And everything spins around
Until that day
When you're old and gray
And redundant made

You are retired and worn out
Unwanted and thrown out
Without work, there's no pay
And so today
I don't have a say

Can't get a job
Can't pay the bills
Can't get credit
Can't afford to live
And sadly can't afford to die

The Victim

The victim stands alone
As she tries to appear strong

The victim stands alone
As she holds her head up high

The victim stands alone
As she has nowhere to turn

The victim stands alone
As she has no one to care

The victim stands alone
But she holds one silent prayer

The victim stands alone
That she's in His tender care

Mother Knows

Mother knows best
When things get stubborn and food is
    short

Mother knows best
When the hamper is empty and how to
    stretch

Mother knows best
How to tighten her belt she gets us the
    best

Mother knows best
She can find a way to fill our bellies with
    lemonade and cake

Mother knows best
When we are at rest, she takes her time
    to sew my dress

Mother knows best
She spends time I confess
To make our lives easier and not
    distressed

Don't Tell Me

Don't tell me I'm here for no reason

Tell me my life has no meaning

That I can make no difference

Don't tell me I'm here for no reason

And only for a while,

And I'm adding to the confusion

Don't tell me I'm here for no reason

When my child is curled up in my
    arms

Depending on me for rhyme and
    reason

Never Stops Ringing

My phone never stops ringing
My phone always gets text messages
From people that I owe and don't know

Stop ringing. Stop texting
Stop sending me messages
Leave me be
I have no money to pay
Stop calling me

With every ring, my heart skips a beat
With every text my pressure goes up
Stop ringing. Stop texting
Leave me be

OK! Here is all I have
Would you like a slice of my soul to go
    with that?
Can't you understand?
Leave me be
Stop ringing me

The Night Walk

It's three in the morning
And I can't sleep
Seems ungrateful to be awake
When others are asleep

Worrying about something
I can't put my finger on
I have no troubles to speak of
There's food and drink and
    somewhere to lay my head

Why then am I wondering?
Back and forth to the kitchen
In the dark, before dawn
Wondering what it is I want
And settling for food.

Why am I awake waiting for the
    dawn?
The children are asleep
Everything is fine
So why am I awake?

Desire

"WHAT EACH KISS MEANS"

- Kiss on the Forehead: We are cute together.
- Kiss on the Cheek: We are friends.
- Kiss on the Hand: I adore you.
- Kiss on the Neck: I want you, now.
- Kiss on the Shoulder: You are perfect.
- Kiss on the Lips: I LOVE YOU...

Stand Under My Umbrella

Waiting in the rain for your train
Wanting to explain away my pain
As you step down from the train
Eger to see you again
Stand under my umbrella

Unable to move I see you
You walk toward me for all to see
You smile. I wave. How sweet.
Stand under my umbrella

Beneath my umbrella
Steamy warm breath rises
Shoulder to shoulder thighs touching
Arms linked we sway together
Stand under my umbrella

Walking down the street
We part, as we meet
You home to your wife me back to
    the street
Our eyes moisten with desire
Ashamed of our deceit
We will meet again tomorrow
Stay under my umbrella

Whisper to Me

Whisper to me softly, sweetly
   whilst my heart is completely open

Whisper to me, whilst my senses soar
   and fly toward you

Whisper to me, let my heart beat faster

Soothe my tangled mind, but be kind

Whisper to me dear, sweet things
   Of love and desire

Whisper to me now, of your hearts
   Desire
Make me your heart's desire

Now whisper, whisper, whisper.

She Doesn't See Me

She sits at her desk shuffling papers

Reading reports and sorting the mail

She doesn't see me

I'm around her every day

Close enough to smell her perfume

I inhale deeply to last me all day

She doesn't see me

If I drum up the courage to tell her,
  how I feel

She may refuse me

No, its better she doesn't see me

The Wish

I wish I were who you think I am
today
But I'm not

I wish I were the girl you married
    years ago
But I'm not

Even the wife you had ten years ago
But I'm not

You must understand that your
    image of me is not who I am
Your dream is not about the real me

Think, who am I?
Think who I will be tomorrow
Think who I will be next year

Step into my reality, try again
Try to remember me as me before
    we were married

Sway Me Through Love

Sway me through love
Help me towards my destiny
Steer me softly with assurance
   of love and life
Hold me tight and sway me
Steer me softly through the misery of
   my wasted life
Sway me through love
Convince me what my love is worth

Sway me on to the end
Keep me there in your arms
Until the end comes
Hold me, squeezed me
Remember me
And when I'm gone
Ensure my memory with your song
Sway me in your memory of love

Hearts of Music

Floating as musical notes your voice
   comes to me
Crossing the fathomless blue green
   waters
Beneath the twilight stars, hanging
   from the dark sky's
Disturbing my restless sleep
I never should have left you

Multi colored bands crossed the
   heavens
Sheltered us as we walked on soft
   cushioned clouds
And lay our heads upon the green
   clover
All this was ours when we were
   together
I never should have left you

Storm clouds gathered, your arms
   grew cold
And darkness filled my heart for your
   coldness was unreal
I withdrew from you and all was lost
I never should have left you

Pain

"We must all suffer one of two things: the pain of discipline or the pain of regret or disappointment".

Jim Rohn

Never Call You

I will never call you
Call you again
To tell you of my pain

Pain so indescribable
Spreading so coldly through my veins

I will never call you again
To complain of my pain

I have thought you
As my only avenue of comfort
I will never call you again

As the pain swarms through my body
    and twists my bones
I will never call you again

Where Are You?

Where are you
I search here and there
Hoping to catch a glimpse
Of your tall frame

I call you by name
Yet you elude me
Do you only exist in my mind?
Or are you a sign

A sign of what is to come
Of the empty years ahead of me
Of my sorrow and discontent
Where are you?

Slip quietly back into my life
As if, you had never left
Uttering sweet words of content
To fill my life again

Where are you?
My sweet, sweet dreamlike
Unmistakably mine
But where are you?

Leave Me Alone

Leave me alone
To cry or die
My tears and my hurts are mine

You hurt me so bad
I hate that you can
Tears scald my eyes
As I blink and wipe my nose

Leave me alone
You hurt me so much
Over and over
My eyes swollen shut
Unexpectedly, I can hardly see
Or even believe this poor creature is
    me

Leave me alone
As I wipe my eyes with my fingers
And put my glasses back on.
My head pounds with anger and
    shame
Knowing that you can still hurt me
    again, and again

Don't Stand

Don't stand upon my heart

Don't take it apart

Hold it gently, closely to your heart

Don't tear it from my bosom

Ease my pain for gain

For the love in my hearts is constant

Without half truths and lies

I bring you pure and untainted love

To be cherished and adored

No swinging door

No in. No out

Only this solemn promise

That my love will endure.

Wings of Time

As the wings of time float quietly past
    her window
She reflects on her gaunt life
Few have tried to placate her
Or raise her from her melancholy

Now in the winter of her life
She drags herself through the
    calendar of her remaining time
With tears of blood dredging through
    her veins
Her fingers fall from the canvas of her
    past deeds
Unable to capture what her blind eyes
    see

What truth her fingers feel
As they bend back to her wrists in
    pain
These are the days of her affliction
As foretold, they will be hers forever

As the remaining time she has winds
    down
To its eventual end of loneliness and
    dismay

Pink Toes

The rain was falling hard and wet

When we made our way to see
    grandpa

And grandpa was so pleased before

He took a look at me

He set Sara on the tabletop

And wiped her muddy feet

Quickly I scrambled up beside her

And took my seat

We giggled and laughed

As the friends we are

As grandpa rinsed her pretty feet

And dried them tenderly

Pink Toes

He took her down from the tabletop

As I slithered to her spot

But there was no rinsing of my pretty
feet

Or tender drying there.

He merely pointed to the pipe

Then to me, then the street

And as we walked home

And I looked down at our feet

Side by side, mine bronze hers pink

The same size, the same feet

But my feet were still muddy

On this wet and muddy street

A Sinners Prayer

Don't let me die alone, Oh Lord

Not even if my sins deserve it

Don't let me die alone

Be merciful to me oh Lord

In my hour of need

Don't let me die alone

Forgive my sins of pride and all

But please

Don't let me die alone

Hope

"Everything that is done in the world is done by hope".

Martin Luther

Three Doors Down

Three doors down from my life

That's where she found me

She was too strong not to fight

She knew what was right

She did not care to sit tight

We'll soon be out of sight

She closed the door tight

Three doors down, we took our flight

I Am Looking

I'm looking for the African in me
That shines through the clear skin
The straight nose
The penciled cheekbones
And the soft wavy hair
That some see

I'm looking for the African in me,
Which depicts the dark skin?
The broad nose
The thick lips
The kink in my hair
These, others see

I'm looking for the African in me
That blends with me
That completes me
That cannot be disguised in me
That accepts me for me
That I see

The Christmas Spirit

The Christmas spirit has always been
with me
And always will be
No matter what happens
I will always be a Christmas person

So bring on the cake
Bring on the ham
Bring on the Christmas feast
For all of these things are Christmas
trappings
That we use to celebrate, His birth

Use this day as the beginning of every
day of the year
Where you show as He has shown you
The love you have for humanity
Not just your man but all men

Love the life you have
And bring to life the life of others

Christmas Is a Coming

Christmas a come, Christmas a come!
It's only three months away
Never mind about today, I have
  things to do
Things to buy in Montego Bay

Christmas a come, Christmas a come
It's only two months away, I've made
  my list
For cake, for gifts and made my plan
  to pay

Christmas has come Christmas has
  come
I lost my job last week
Children have to go back to school

One chicken and bread we have to
  eat
No cake. No presents as planed
But Christmas still a charm
And the church will be crammed
An excitement still in the air
New Year has come. New Year has
  come! Oh well, back to square one

Santa's Mail

Ring Ring, Ring Ring,
Hello, is this Santa?
This is your virtual assistant calling.
I have a gazillion messages for you.

I'm so sorry, I know its Boxing Day.
But there was a mix-up with you and
    that other guy
Do you think you could do a quick rain-
    deer run? It's very important

Hey, there's no need for that kind of
    talk.
I'm only a virtual assistant after all.
By the way, I did not get a gift this year
And why would I be on the naughty list?
You have all your messages now

I Am Blessed

Every day I know that I am blessed
And that angels watch over me
While I sleep
While I walk and talk
And with every word I speak
Angels watch over me

Throw your arms around me
While I pray each night
And keep me safe from harm
As love expounds and swells in me
For all who surround me each day

This gift of love we all possess
Is truly a gift from heaven
To be shared repeatedly
And I will hold on to it forever

The angels are watching over me
Today and forever
As I keep on living day by day
Keeping love in my heart for others
Whatever I may weather
As each day angels watch over me

Any Day Now

I will keep quiet
I will not say a word

Because I am going to be, free
Free to see the Lord in all His glory

I will keep quiet
And not say a word

I will have no evil thoughts,
Or pursue any evil deed,

I am going to be, free.
Any day now

Free to see my Lord

Death

"Every man must do two things alone; he must do his own believing and his own dying".

Martin Luther

My Baby Sleeps

Steadily, steadily I rock my baby to
    sleep
I hush her wailing heart
And soothe her till she sleeps

Her little chest heaves from the pangs of
    cold and hunger
Ultimately, my quest is to make her
    slumber

She will never wake again
For I have made sure
She will endure no more.

She sleeps serenely in my aching arms
Such a sweet, sweet smile

Pain will no longer be hers to bear
As she has gone
Somewhere without a care

The Zombie

The second knock on the door is
    what we're waiting for

To seal our fate, I can hardly wait
For your embrace

In your haste, we find a spot to get
    real hot
But we had to stop

For the second knock on the door
Was more than we thought

Charging headlong into the store.
She came.
Without fanfare or shame
Shouting and screaming

With one shot
We ended her pain
And started again
Still waiting for
The second knock on the door.

Could Not Wait

I could not wait for death

Though it was not far behind

I still took the next step

Onward, hurrying through the night

Onward until morning light

I shall not wait for death tonight

Do You Hear The Bells?

Hearts beating on sacred ground
Do you hear the bells?

Anxiously, we wander on
Do you hear the bells?

Searching for the telltale signs
Of those who died and were left
    behind
Do you hear the bells?

Compelled tonight when the moon is
    right
To stretch their twisted limbs to its
    light
Do you hear the bells?

Squirming from their graves
To view the moon in her silver gown
Steadily they stumble toward
That which summons them forth
Do you hear the bells?

As Butterflies Flutter

I like to see the butterflies fluttering
    by
And the bees buzzing here and there

As the hot cement street beneath my
    feet
Gradually warm my heavy limbs

Looking up as passersby gather nearer

I am unable to speak

my breath becomes weak

As my heart misses a beat

Oh, I like to see butterflies fluttering by.

Limericks

Dot

There once was a baby called Dot
Who thought she could handle the pot
She sidled up to it and made sure she
used it
But bungled it when she got off it.

E.P.A.F.

MUM

There once was a lad in the army
Who thought that his mum was quite
barmy
He wrote her a note in hopes of a quote
But instead, he got day old baloney

E.P.A.F.

Printed in Great Britain
by Amazon.co.uk, Ltd.,
Marston Gate.